HAL•LEONARD

VIOLIN PLAY-ALONG

BROADWAY HITS

CONTENTS

ISBN 978-1-61780-776-3

Recorded and Produced at
Beathouse Music, Milwaukee, WI

Violin by Jerry Loughney

HAL•LEONARD®
CORPORATION

7777 W. BLUEMOUND RD. P.O. BOX 13819 MILWAUKEE, WI 53213

Visit Hal Leonard Online at
www.halleonard.com

Dancing Queen

from MAMMA MIA!

Words and Music by BENNY ANDERSSON,
BJÖRN ULVAEUS and STIG ANDERSON

Castle on a Cloud

from LES MISÉRABLES

Music by CLAUDE-MICHEL SCHÖNBERG
Lyrics by ALAIN BOUBLIL, JEAN-MARC NATEL
and HERBERT KRETZMER

Defying Gravity

from the Broadway Musical WICKED

Music and Lyrics by
STEPHEN SCHWARTZ

Fiddler on the Roof

from the Musical FIDDLER ON THE ROOF

Words by SHELDON HARNICK
Music by JERRY BOCK

My Favorite Things

from THE SOUND OF MUSIC

Lyrics by OSCAR HAMMERSTEIN II
Music by RICHARD RODGERS

I Whistle a Happy Tune

from THE KING AND I

Lyrics by OSCAR HAMMERSTEIN II
Music by RICHARD RODGERS

On My Own

from LES MISÉRABLES

Music by CLAUDE-MICHEL SCHÖNBERG
Lyrics by ALAIN BOUBLIL, JEAN-MARC NATEL,
HERBERT KRETZMER, JOHN CAIRD
and TREVOR NUNN

Put On a Happy Face

from BYE BYE BIRDIE

Lyric by LEE ADAMS
Music by CHARLES STROUSE